Once upon a time a child like you
made a PATCHWORK BLOCK
and this is how!
Would you like to make one now?

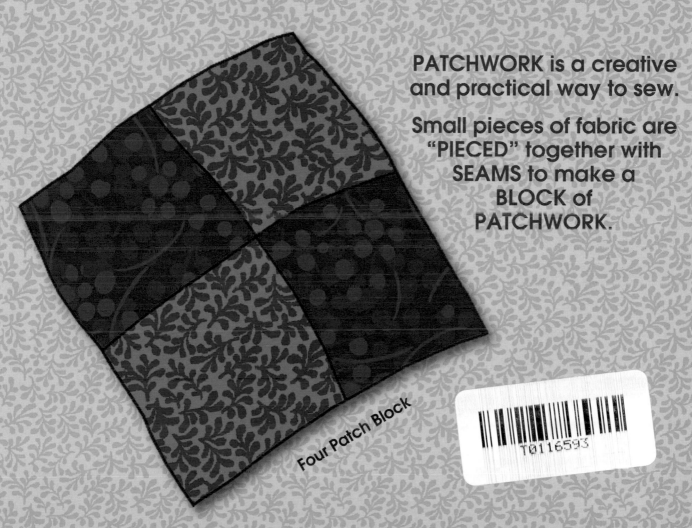

PATCHWORK is a creative
and practical way to sew.

Small pieces of fabric are
"PIECED" together with
SEAMS to make a
BLOCK of
PATCHWORK.

Four Patch Block

RULES FOR PATCHWORK

1. MAKE SMALL PROJECTS WITH BIG PIECES FIRST. Setting limits helps you finish what you start and learn something new.

2. USE SHAPES with SQUARE CORNERS and STRAIGHT LINES. Make edges and cross seams match on simple shapes first.

3. WORK ON A FLAT SURFACE, so you can lay the pieces flat. Make sure it is clean and neat.

4. USE RECOMMENDED SUPPLIES. Buy 100% cotton woven fabric for PATCHWORK projects. Read the labels on the fabric bolts.

5. USE AN IRON TO PRESS FABRIC FLAT BEFORE TRACING PATCHWORK SHAPES ON FABRIC.

6. USE a PERFECT TEMPLATE to mark and cut PERFECT FABRIC PIECES.

7. PLACE the OUTSIDE EDGE of a PERFECT TEMPLATE along a STRAIGHT THREAD LINE when marking pieces for PATCHWORK design.

8. USE A MASKING TAPE SEAM GUIDE to make ALL of the SEAM ALLOWANCES THE SAME SIZE. Measure and stitch accurately.

9. USE AN IRON TO PRESS PATCHWORK SEAM ALLOWANCES in one direction, usually toward the darker fabric.

10. FIX MISTAKES. Undo and restitch seams that have tiny tucks or that do not match at cross seams.

11. USE A CHECKLIST TO SEW. A list helps you remember what to do.

12. FINISH YOUR WORK. Do not begin something new until you complete what you started to do.

SECOND EDITION

The Winky Cherry System
OF TEACHING YOUNG CHILDREN TO SEW

My First Machine* Patchwork Book SEWING PROJECTS

* plus some hand-sewing options

by Winky Cherry
edited by Linda Wisner, Jeannette Schilling, Pati Palmer, and Ann Gosch
designed by Linda Wisner

This book belongs to

_____

A Letter to Parents, Teachers and Grown-ups:

Patchwork, a craft with ancient and modern history, has evolved into a contemporary creative hobby and an American folk art. Pieces of fabric are "pieced" together with seams. Designs have names that provide a record of personal memories and historical events. We continue to reproduce and rearrange these fabric blocks with a sense of satisfaction that can only be described by doing it.

I have been teaching boys and girls sewing skills and, as a result, life skills, for almost 40 years. ***My First Machine Patchwork Book***, the fifth level in **The Winky Cherry System of Teaching Young Children to Sew**™ series, introduces patchwork to beginners as they make a four patch block by machine (or by hand). The sequence of construction is as important as the finished work. This book introduces the iron as a sewing tool and teaches a beginner to use a seam guide. The patchwork projects in this book use the traditional ¼" seam allowances. Some young beginners may find it easier to sew with a ½" seam allowance. When children understand elementary patchwork math and can make an accurate ½" measurement consistently, they are ready to use a traditional ¼" patchwork seam allowance.

The first part of patchwork is getting ready to sew by choosing the project, gathering supplies, preparing the fabric, and using a template with a seam allowance to make fabric patches. Stitching and pressing is the second part. Checklists for stitching seams help the child remember to make consistent seam allowances and to match seams that cross. The third part of patchwork is practicing to improve skills.

Alphabet code flags provide a simple patchwork block for each letter of the alphabet to make into pillows or flags, or to save to make a quilt.

My First Quilt Book, the next in this series, uses nine 10" patchwork blocks to make a quilt. If the child has not yet learned to use a sewing machine, we recommend starting with the previous book in this series, ***My First Sewing Machine Book***, to introduce children to making projects with a sewing machine.

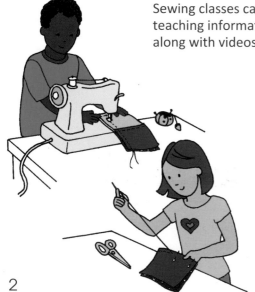

Sewing classes can be built around each of the six books in this series. I have developed teaching information, which is available from Palmer/Pletsch at **www.palmerpletsch.com**, along with videos for both teachers and children.

Winky Cherry

Winky Cherry

Second Edition copyright © 2016 by Palmer/Pletsch Publishing
Original copyright © 1997.
Illustrations by Jeannette Schilling, Kate Pryka, and Linda Wisner

Published by Palmer/Pletsch Publishing,
www.palmerpletsch.com
Printed in the USA

ISBN 978-0-935278-89-7

PATCHWORK BLOCKS HAVE NAMES

Many PATCHWORK BLOCKS were named by people who made them a long time ago.

Simple names come from the design of shapes and colors inside the BLOCKS you sew.

Some BLOCK names tell stories of life, nature, religion, history, common things and places.

Patchwork made from pieces of a wedding dress or outgrown clothes holds memories of special times and faces.

The first American flag was pieced with strips and appliquéd with stars.

Roman Stripe

Double Four Patch

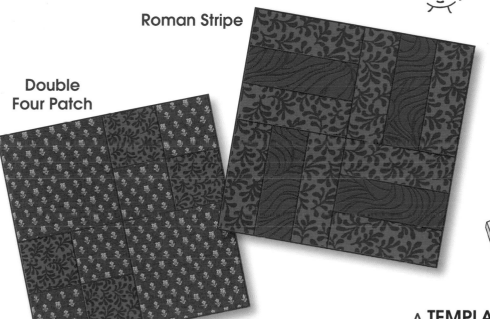

A **TEMPLATE** is a pattern for one piece in a BLOCK. It is made of plastic or poster board.

The first PATCHWORK TEMPLATES were made of wood or tin.

5

THINGS YOU WILL NEED:

- ❐ **5¹/₂" template** comes in book kit or **to make one, see page 7-9**
- ❐ **alphabet block patterns** (see page 38)
- ❐ **pincushion** with strawberry to sharpen the needle
- ❐ **pencil**   ❐ **straight pins**
- ❐ **needle**   ❐ **special pin**
- ❐ **sewing machine** for machine stitching
- ❐ **thread** cotton thread
- ❐ **scissors** for cutting fabric AND another pair for cutting paper or poster board
- ❐ **snippers** for cutting THREAD
- ❐ **iron**
- ❐ **ironing board**
- ❐ **sandpaper #5**
- ❐ **masking tape** as a sewing machine seam guide
- ❐ **100% cotton woven fabrics**
    - two to four prints for Four Patch Block (page 10)
    - various prints to make more blocks (page 31)
    - red, blue, yellow, white and black solids for the alphabet code flags (page 35)

You may also ask your local quilt store to recommend their favorite quilting tools.

fabric scissors

paper scissors

6

MAKE A TEMPLATE

Trace this shape onto template plastic or poster board and follow the directions on the next two pages.

NOTE:
A 5¹/₂" poster board template for the Four Patch Block is included in the kit.

CUT HERE
to create a 5¹/₂-inch template with a 1/4" seam allowance. This line matches the 5¹/₂" template included in the kit and the instructions in this book.

CUT HERE
to create a 6-inch template with a 1/2" seam allowance. (See note on page 8.)

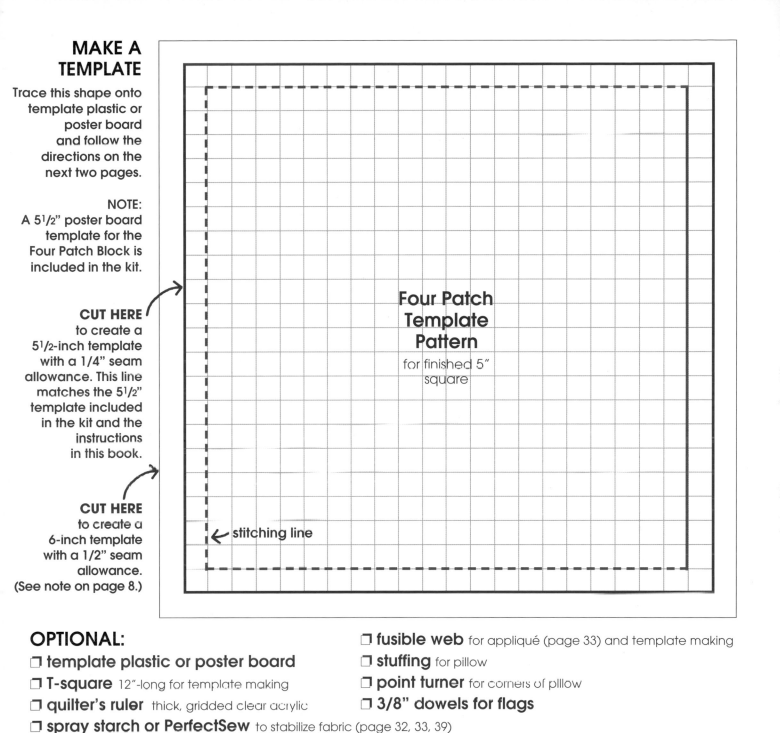

Four Patch
Template
Pattern
for finished 5"
square

← stitching line

OPTIONAL:

❒ **template plastic or poster board**
❒ **T-square** 12"-long for template making
❒ **quilter's ruler** thick, gridded clear acrylic
❒ **spray starch or PerfectSew** to stabilize fabric (page 32, 33, 39)

❒ **fusible web** for appliqué (page 33) and template making
❒ **stuffing** for pillow
❒ **point turner** for corners of pillow
❒ **3/8" dowels for flags**

MAKE TEMPLATES FOR THE FOUR PATCH BLOCK

A TEMPLATE IS A PATTERN FOR PATCHWORK SHAPES.

1. Place a SQUARE CORNER of clear template plastic or poster board on top of a SQUARE CORNER on the TEMPLATE drawing on page 7.

2. TRACE the TEMPLATE. Use a pencil and a T-square or ruler to make STRAIGHT lines and SQUARE CORNERS.

Traditionally, quilters sew using 1/4" seam allowances. The illustrations in this book show 1/4" seam allowances.

NOTE: When you are first learning, 1/2" seam allowances *might* be easier for you. If you choose to use 1/2" seam allowances, start with a 6" template.

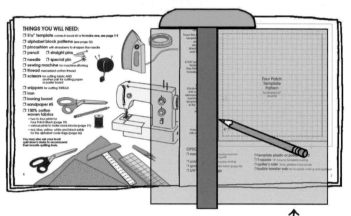

Clear template plastic is easiest to use.

3. Cut out the TEMPLATE. (Use your paper scissors, not your good fabric scissors!)

AFTER YOU MAKE YOUR FOUR PATCH BLOCK, MAKE TEMPLATES FOR OTHER SIZES.

10" square plus 1/4" seam allowances

5" x 10" plus 1/4" seam allowances

10" x 3 1/3" plus 1/4" seam allowances

Keep all the TEMPLATES for ONE BLOCK in ONE envelope or plastic bag, labeled with the BLOCK'S NAME.

You can stitch a shape onto a square. See page 33 for appliqué directions.

MAKE YOUR OWN TEMPLATES

TO MAKE YOUR OWN PLASTIC OR POSTER BOARD TEMPLATE:

1. Use a T-square to measure from one side of a SQUARE CORNER of the template material. Make a pencil mark.

2. Use the T-square to measure the same distance from the OTHER SIDE of the SAME SQUARE CORNER and make a SECOND pencil mark.

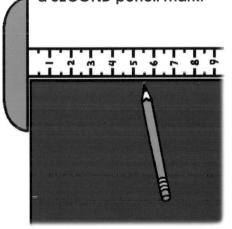

3. Move the T-square to draw a straight line from the FIRST pencil mark at least as long as the template will be.

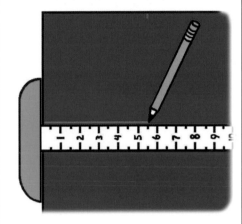

4. Move the T-square to draw a straight line from the SECOND pencil mark to make a square.

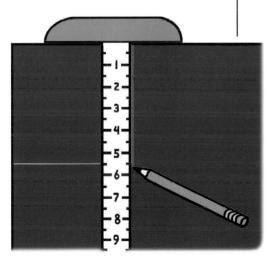

5. Cut out the TEMPLATE carefully to make a perfect square.

Do patchwork math to find out what size the template needs to be. For the four patch block in this book, make a 5 1/2" template.

Learning GEOMETRY will help you make TEMPLATES for any shape you want to sew. MATH is important to know.

9

Getting ready is the FIRST PART of MAKING A PATCHWORK BLOCK. Are you ready to start?

GET READY STEP 1

CHOOSE A PATCHWORK BLOCK

A BLOCK with four squares is an easy-to-sew design with SQUARE CORNERS and STRAIGHT LINES.

The shapes inside THIS BLOCK give it the name FOUR PATCH.

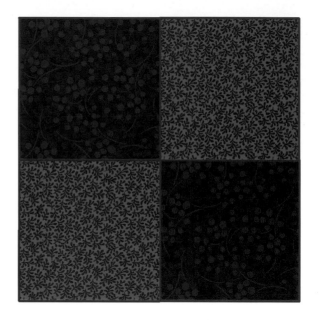

PATCHWORK MATH IS MEASURING AND PLANNING
the size of the BLOCK,
the size of the PIECES,
and the size of the SEAM ALLOWANCE.

PLAN THE SIZE OF THE BLOCK

THE SIZE OF A FINISHED PROJECT DOES NOT INCLUDE SEAM ALLOWANCES.

A 5½" fabric square sewn with a 1/4" seam allowance will make a 5" FINISHED square.

Four 5½" fabric squares sewn with a 1/4" seam allowance will make a 10" FINISHED FOUR PATCH BLOCK.

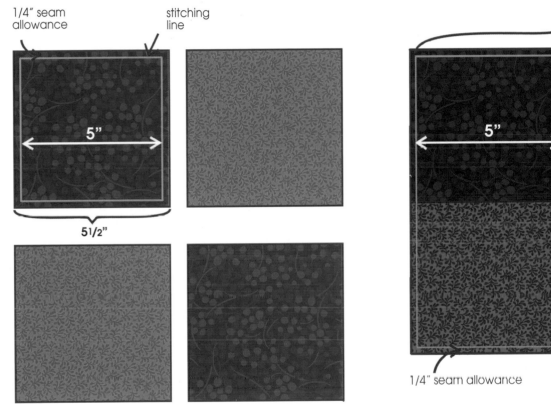

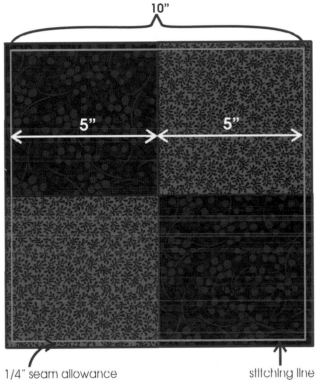

A **SEAM ALLOWANCE** is the space between the stitching and the edge of the fabric. Patchwork is commonly sewn using 1/4" seam allowances.

CHOOSE THE FABRIC

USE **100% COTTON WOVEN** FABRIC.

Choose four different fabrics OR...choose two.

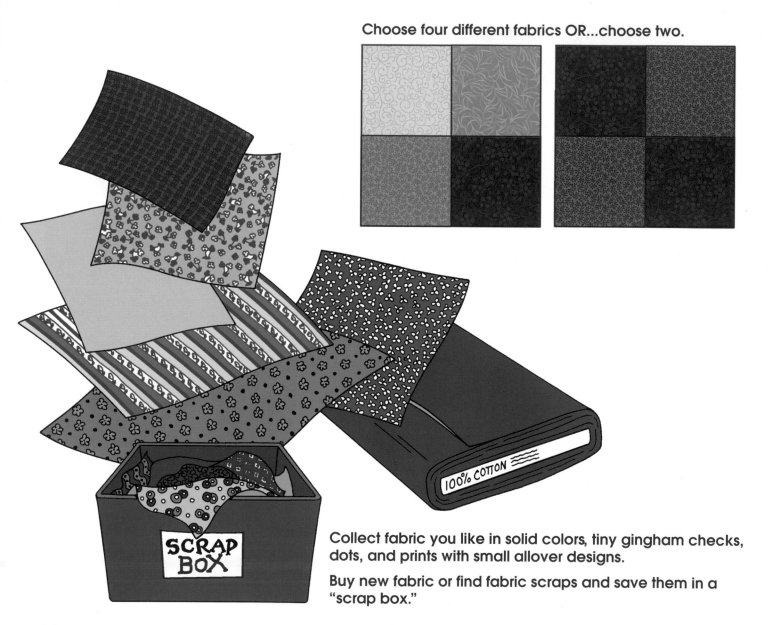

Collect fabric you like in solid colors, tiny gingham checks, dots, and prints with small allover designs.

Buy new fabric or find fabric scraps and save them in a "scrap box."

PREPARE THE FABRIC

WASH AND DRY THE FABRIC.

Learning to WASH and DRY fabric
is PART OF LEARNING TO SEW.
IF SOMEONE DOES IT FOR YOU
YOU WON'T LEARN WHAT TO DO.

Washing fabric before you sew
is important because some
fabrics BLEED (lose color) or
SHRINK (get smaller) when
they get wet.

Mr. Tuck and Ms. Wrinkle
will help remind you to
be careful not to make
boo-boos.

13

USE AN IRON TO PRESS THE FABRIC

AN IRON IS A TOOL WITH SAFETY RULES.

Plug in the IRON before you use it, and unplug it when you are through. FOLLOW THE RULES for using an IRON and be careful when you do.

nose

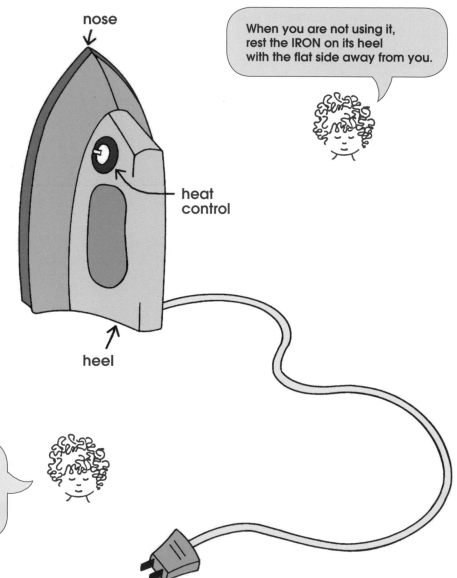

When you are not using it, rest the IRON on its heel with the flat side away from you.

heat control

heel

TEST THE TEMPERATURE.

READ the HEAT CONTROL on the IRON to find the temperature setting for the fabric you are using.

SET the dial for COTTON FABRIC.

CHECK TO SEE IF THE IRON IS HOT.

Press the IRON to the ironing board.

Stand the iron on its heel and feel the spot.

If the IRON is too hot it can burn the fabric. If the IRON is too cool it won't press out the wrinkles to make the fabric FLAT.

14

IRON THE FABRIC TO MAKE IT FLAT

Iron on the WRONG SIDE of the fabric to keep the RIGHT SIDE of the fabric fresh and new.
The IRON can burn, shine or dull fabric, if you're not careful what you do.

Keep the hand not holding the iron safe behind your back and out of the way when you are moving the iron, or wear a glove on that hand.

PUSH MS. WRINKLE AWAY!
FLAT fabric pieces are easy to measure, cut and sew.

Learn to make appliqué patches on page 331

USE A TEMPLATE TO DRAW FOUR SQUARES ON FABRIC

PLACE THE TEMPLATE.

On the **WRONG SIDE** of the fabric place a **STRAIGHT EDGE** of the **TEMPLATE** along a **STRAIGHT THREAD** in the woven fabric.

> Use masking tape to tape **SANDPAPER** to the table, rough side up. Use it under the fabric to keep the fabric from moving when you draw.

DRAW AROUND THE TEMPLATE.

Use a pencil to draw around the edges of the template to mark the **CUTTING LINE**.

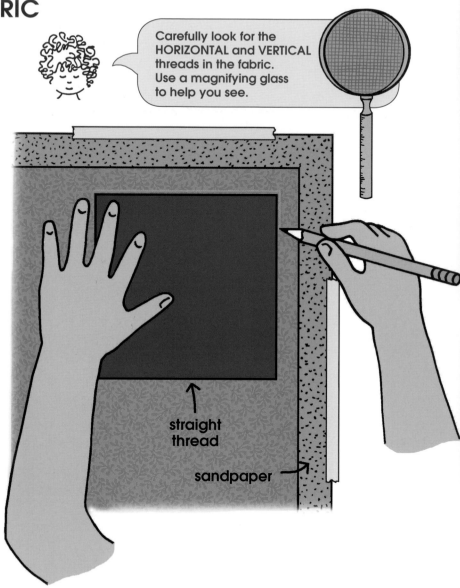

> Carefully look for the **HORIZONTAL** and **VERTICAL** threads in the fabric. Use a magnifying glass to help you see.

straight thread

sandpaper

Cut carefully along each pencil line.

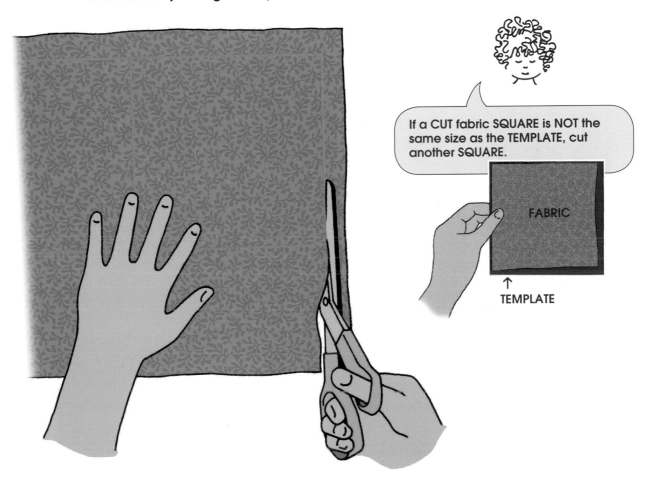

If a CUT fabric SQUARE is NOT the same size as the TEMPLATE, cut another SQUARE.

FABRIC

↑
TEMPLATE

LAY OUT THE BLOCK

PLACE THE FOUR CUT SQUARES TO LOOK LIKE THE FOUR PATCH BLOCK.

Put the four fabric squares RIGHT SIDE UP to see
where you want each square in the BLOCK to be.

NUMBER THE SQUARES
Write a number in pencil on the back of each fabric square
to show how to place them when you sew them together
to make the FOUR PATCH block.

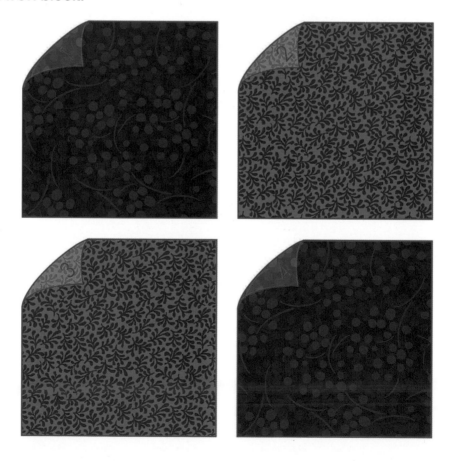

ROW #1

ROW #2

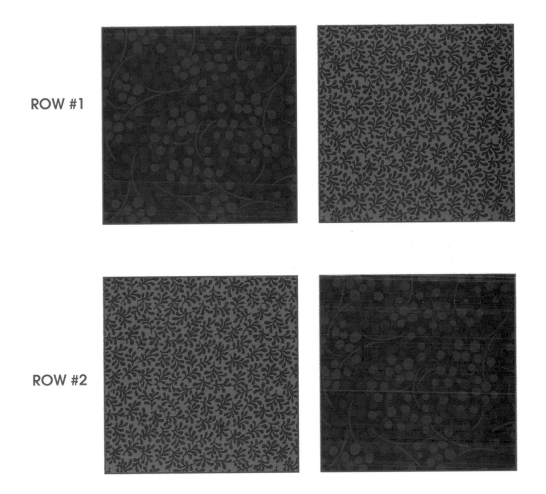

FLIP SQUARE #2 ONTO SQUARE #1

Pick up SQUARE #2, TURN IT OVER, and PLACE the RIGHT SIDE DOWN on top of SQUARE #1.

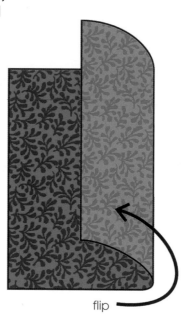

flip

DRAW THE SEAM LINE ON THE FABRIC

A seam guide helps you make all the seam allowances the same size.

To make a seam guide:

Use a ruler, a pencil and scissors to make a strip of poster board or template plastic that is the width of your seam allowance and as long as the block.

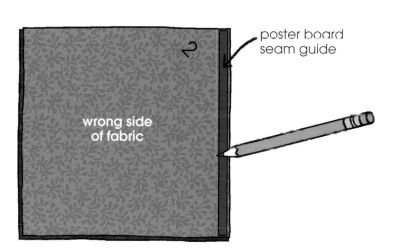

poster board seam guide

wrong side of fabric

PIN THE SQUARES TOGETHER

MATCH the edges of the fabric carefully and place pin points out and pin heads in.

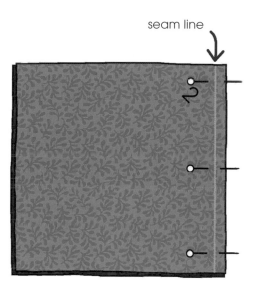

seam line

21

STITCHING and PRESSING is the SECOND PART OF MAKING A PATCHWORK BLOCK.

TO STITCH BY HAND

GET A NEEDLE AND THREAD READY TO SEW.

Thread the needle, pull the threads even, and make a knot.

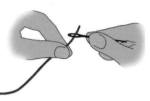

USE RUNNING STITCHES.

Make down and up stitches 1/8" apart on the LINE.
The KNOT on the end of the thread locks the stitches.
At the end of the seam, remember to LOCK the stitches too.

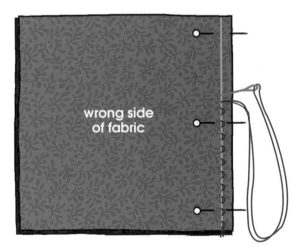

wrong side of fabric

My First Sewing Book taught you to make SAVE-THE-LOOP LOCK STITCHES.
If you don't remember go back and take a look.

If you are sewing by hand, skip the next page.

PLACE **SEAM GUIDE TAPE** ON THE MACHINE.

Put a PIECE of MASKING TAPE 1/4" from the NEEDLE to mark the 1/4" SEAM ALLOWANCE space between the stitches and the matched edges.

STITCH THE SEAM.

Set the machine to sew eight to ten stitches per inch.

Put the pinned squares under the NEEDLE with the pins pointing to the tape.

Guide the MATCHED EDGES along the TAPE and go slow to make all SEAM ALLOWANCES the same size as you sew.

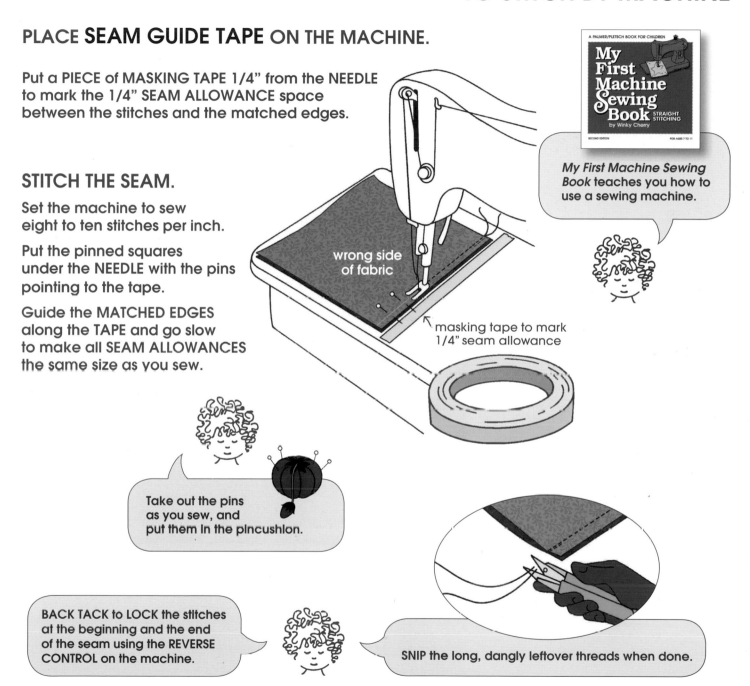

wrong side of fabric

↖ masking tape to mark 1/4" seam allowance

My First Machine Sewing Book teaches you how to use a sewing machine.

Take out the pins as you sew, and put them In the pincushion.

BACK TACK to LOCK the stitches at the beginning and the end of the seam using the REVERSE CONTROL on the machine.

SNIP the long, dangly leftover threads when done.

PRESS THE SEAM ALLOWANCE

Place the stitched fabric SQUARES on the ironing board. If one fabric is darker than the other, place the darker fabric on top.

Press to SET THE STITCHES.

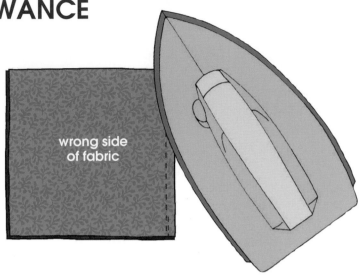

wrong side of fabric

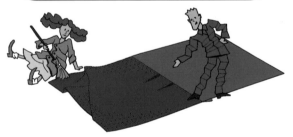

PRESS FLAT carefully. Ms. Wrinkle likes to make the fabric look wrinkly!

Mr. Tuck likes to make folds in the fabric when you press or stitch. These are sewing problems that YOU must fix!

Flip the top SQUARE over to lie flat on the ironing board and use the iron to PRESS the SQUARES and SEAM ALLOWANCES FLAT.

If one fabric is darker than the other, the SEAM ALLOWANCES should be under the darker side.

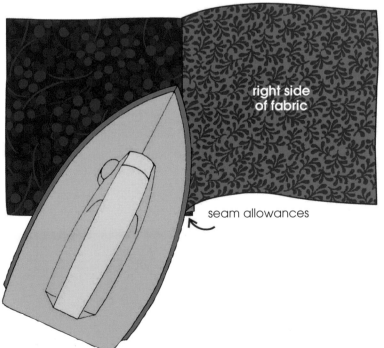

right side of fabric

seam allowances

STITCHING CHECKLIST

☑ **LAY OUT pieces in rows, RIGHT SIDE UP.**
Make two rows with two squares in each row.

Use a CHECKLIST to remind yourself what to do.

☑ **Get ready to stitch.**
1. PUT RIGHT SIDES of two squares TOGETHER.
2. Mark SEAM LINES on wrong side of fabric.
3. MATCH EDGES.
4. PIN. Place pin points out and heads in.

☑ **SEW the seam.**
1. USE A MASKING TAPE SEAM GUIDE on the sewing machine to make all the SEAM ALLOWANCES the same size.
2. BACK TACK to LOCK the stitches at the beginning and the end of the SEAM.
3. CHECK the front and the back of the seam for wrinkles and tucks. If there are any tucks, undo the stitches, press the squares, and sew them together again.

☑ **PRESS the SEAM.**
1. PRESS along the stitching line to SET THE STITCHES.
2. PRESS the darker square away from the lighter one on the right side of the fabric.
3. CHECK the front and back of the SEAM for wrinkles and tucks.

LAY OUT ROW #1 AND ROW #2, RIGHT SIDES UP

Place the rows so the seams line up
and the two squares of the same fabric
are not next to each other.

ROW #1

ROW #2

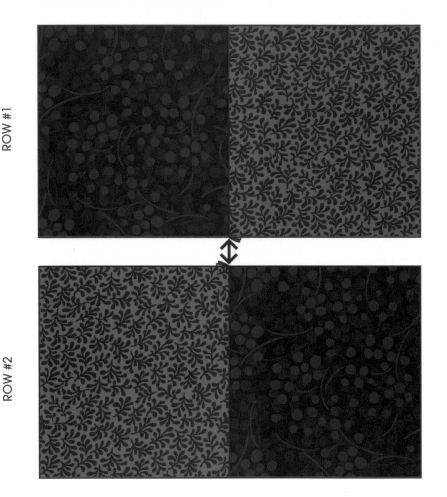

Find SEAMS that CROSS
on the clothes you wear.
Look at the SEAMS
   under your arms.
Do you see CROSS SEAMS there?

FLIP, MATCH EDGES, AND PIN THE LONG SEAM

PLACE ONE **SPECIAL PIN** TO HOLD THE CROSS SEAMS MATCHED.

YOU decide what pin wlll be YOUR SPECIAL PIN.
It will remind you to do something new.

This pin STAYS IN when the stitches go through.

Flip ROW #1 onto ROW #2 RIGHT SIDES TOGETHER, and MATCH THE EDGES.

Poke a **SPECIAL PIN DOWN THROUGH THE STITCHES** on ROW #1 and ROW #2 to HOLD the cross seams matched.

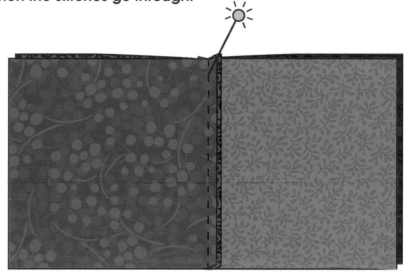

Place two pins to hold the SEAM ALLOWANCES in place and more pins to keep the long edges matched.

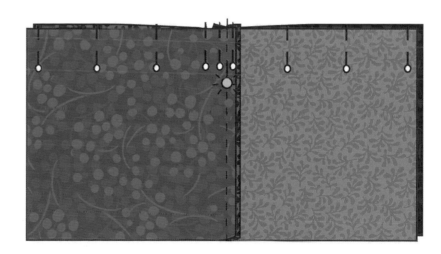

STITCH THE SEAM

PUT THE PINNED ROW UNDER THE NEEDLE WITH PINS POINTING TO THE TAPE.

BACK TACK to LOCK the stitches as you start to sew.
Remember to take the REGULAR PINS out as you go.

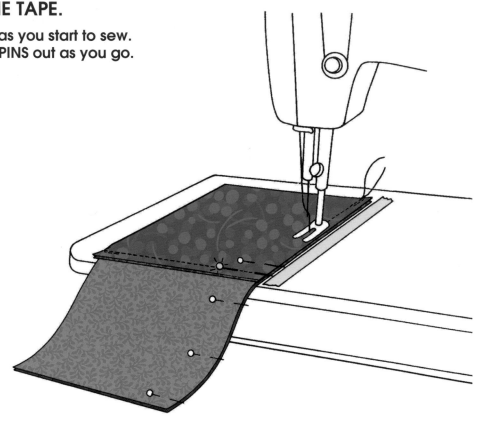

USE YOUR HAND
TO TURN THE WHEEL,
TO WALK THE NEEDLE
OVER THE SPECIAL PIN.

The SPECIAL PIN reminds you
to LEAVE IT IN, to keep the
CROSS SEAMS MATCHED
when stitching.

REMEMBER to LOCK the stitches
at the END of the SEAM too,
and put pins away.

PRESS the LONG SEAM ALLOWANCE TO ONE SIDE

CHECK to see if the CROSS SEAMS MATCH and the SEAM ALLOWANCE is stitched accurately. Undo a boo-boo and REDO the stitches carefully.

TUCKS and UNMATCHED SEAMS are lessons for you. Learn from mistakes. What did you do?

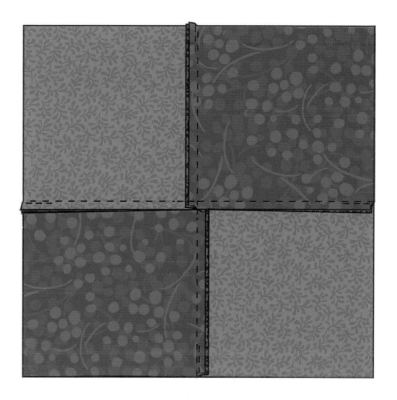

Your first PATCHWORK BLOCK is done.
Do you want to make another one?

To use the BLOCK to make
a PILLOW or a FLAG, turn the page now.

THE THIRD PART OF PATCHWORK IS FINISHING THE BLOCK AS A PILLOW, A FLAG, OR A PART OF A QUILT.

TO MAKE A PILLOW:

1. Cut a BACK for the pillow.
2. Pin the BLOCK and the back right sides together.
3. Use a seam guide as you stitch around all sides, leaving an opening for turning.
4. Trim the corner points.

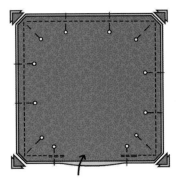

leave open for turning

5. Turn right side out and poke out corner points with a point turner or pencil.
6. Stuff the pillow.
7. Fold the SEAM ALLOWANCE in along the open edge and pin.
8. Overstitch and lockstitch by hand.

TO MAKE A FLAG:

After turning, use a 1/2" seam guide to stitch a seam along the left side of the BLOCK.

Take out the stitches at the bottom to make a hole for a 3/8" wooden dowel flag pole.

Don't stuff the flag!

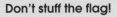

YOU MAY ALSO USE PATCHWORK BLOCKS TO MAKE A QUILT.

My First Quilt Book will show you how. You can learn something new!

A PALMER/PLETSCH BOOK FOR CHILDREN
My First Quilt Book MACHINE SEWING
by Winky Cherry
SECOND EDITION   FOR AGES 7 AND UP

THE FOURTH PART OF PATCHWORK IS PRACTICE.
THE MORE BLOCKS YOU MAKE, THE BETTER YOU SEW!

MAKE BLOCKS WITH SQUARES AND RECTANGLES
the same way you made the FOUR PATCH BLOCK.

Add an APPLIQUÉ PATCH to your blocks!
Page 33 shows you how.

MAKE PATCHWORK BLOCKS WITH TRIANGLES
after you KNOW how to make PATCHWORK BLOCKS with SQUARES and RECTANGLES

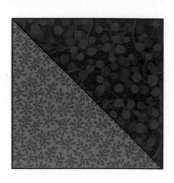

BIAS EDGES STRETCH.

BIAS is the stretchy, diagonal line in woven fabric.

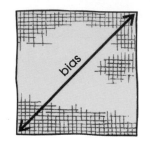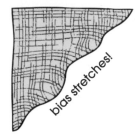

CUT OUTSIDE EDGE ON STRAIGHT THREADS.

The OUTSIDE edges of a BLOCK should NOT be bias. Cut the fabric pieces so the OUTSIDE edges of the block are on a STRAIGHT THREAD.

Use SPRAY STARCH to stiffen fabric to keep bias edges from stretching before drawing, cutting and stitching. IRON the fabric after the stabilizer dries. (PerfectSew works too—ask a grown-up to help you. It is available at palmerpletsch.com)

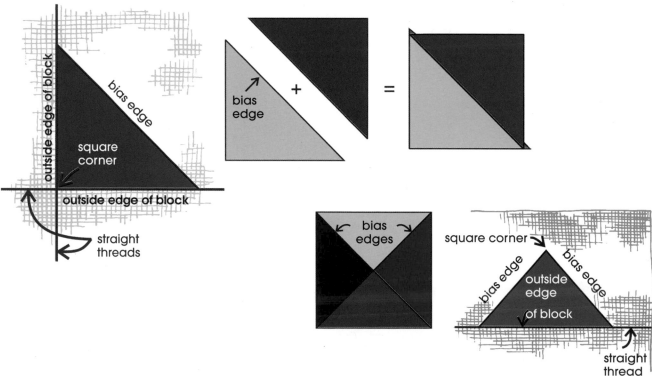

STITCH A SHAPE ON TOP OF A BLOCK

An APPLIQUÉ is a fabric shape stitched on top of a background.

Like triangles, APPLIQUÉ shapes have bias edges. Stiffen the fabric as described on the previous page to make it easier to sew.

MAKE AN APPLIQUÉ BLOCK

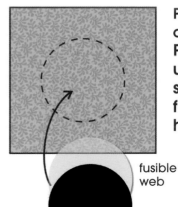

Place a cut-out shape onto a fabric square. Pin in place and/or use fusible web (cut slightly smaller) and fuse with an iron to hold it in place.

fusible web

TO STITCH BY MACHINE:

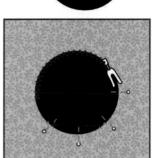

Set your sewing machine to a ZIGZAG (SATIN STITCH). The stitches will cover most of the raw (cut) edges of the fabric.

TO STITCH BY HAND:

Use the running stitch you learned on page 22, or an overstitch like you learned in *My First Sewing Book*.

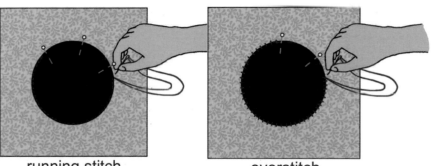

running stitch

overstitch

STITCH PATCHWORK BLOCKS TOGETHER TO MAKE A LARGE 20" BLOCK

Follow directions to make a four patch block. Make four blocks.

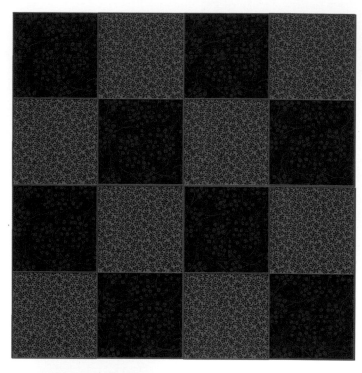

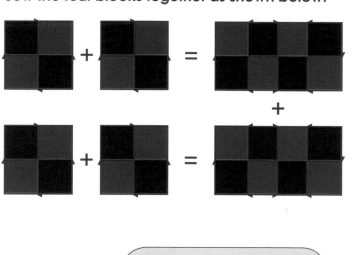

make four of these

Sew the four blocks together as shown below:

> This could be a pillow or a quilt for a doll like the dolls from *My First Doll Book*.

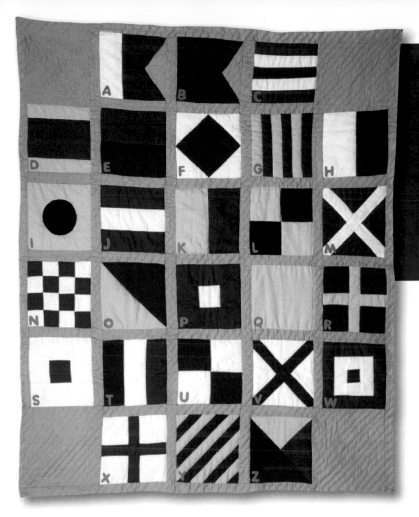

A PATCHWORK BLOCK ALPHABET

This International Code Flag quilt contains blocks that represent the MORSE CODE—a code that sailors, soldiers, pilots, and astronauts use. Each FLAG has a CODE NAME, an IMPORTANT MESSAGE, and a LETTER NAME to use with other flags to write words.

The MORSE CODE is an alphabet of dots (●) and dashes (▬).

THE PLACEMENT OF SHAPES AND COLOR GIVES A BLOCK A NAME.

When the shapes in two blocks are the same, like "H" and "K," THE USE OF COLOR GIVES EACH BLOCK A DIFFERENT NAME.

  "H"

  "K"

A ● ▬
ALPHA

DIVER BELOW. KEEP WELL CLEAR AT LOW SPEED. (Stay away from me and go slowly.)

B ▬ ● ● ●
BRAVO

I AM CARRYING DANGEROUS GOODS. (The things I have on my boat are not safe.)

C ▬ ● ▬ ●
CHARLIE

YES!

D ▬ ● ●
DELTA

KEEP CLEAR OF ME. I AM MOVING WITH DIFFICULTY.

35

E ·
ECHO
I AM ALTERING MY COURSE
TO STARBOARD.
(I'm moving to the right.)

F · · · —
FOXTROT
I AM DISABLED.
COMMUNICATE WITH ME.
(I cannot move. Talk to me.)

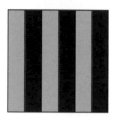

G — — ·
GOLF
I NEED A GUIDE.

H · · · ·
HOTEL
I HAVE A PILOT ON BOARD.
(I have a guide on my boat to
help me go where I want to go.)

I · ·
INDIA
I AM ALTERING MY COURSE
TO PORT.
(I am moving to the left.)

J · — — —
JULIET
I AM ON FIRE;
KEEP CLEAR OF ME.
(I'm burning; stay away.)

K — · —
KILO
I HAVE SOMETHING TO
COMMUNICATE.
(I want to tell you something.)

L · — · ·
LIMA
YOU SHOULD STOP
YOUR VESSEL.
(You need to stop your boat.)

M — — —
MIKE
MY VESSEL IS STOPPED.
(I have stopped my boat.)

N — ·
NOVEMBER
NO!
(Negative)

O — — —
OSCAR
MAN OVERBOARD.
(Someone fell off of the boat.)

When the shapes in two blocks
are the same, the way the shapes are
placed, HORIZONTALLY or VERTICALLY,
gives a BLOCK a name, like "J" and "T."

The instructions for the appliqué circle
for the letter "I" are on page 33.

P · — — ·
PAPA

ALL ABOARD.
(People must
get on the boat.)

Q — — · —
QUEBEC

I REQUEST FREE PRACTIQUE.
(I ask for customs clearance.)

R · — ·
ROMEO

MY MOVEMENT IS RESTRICTED
BECAUSE THE WATER IS NOT
DEEP ENOUGH.

S · · ·
SIERRA

MY ENGINES ARE GOING FULL
SPEED ASTERN. (My boat is
moving backward fast.)

T —
TANGO

KEEP CLEAR OF ME.
(Stay away.)

U · · —
UNIFORM

YOU ARE RUNNING INTO
DANGER. (You are moving
toward a bad area.)

V · · · —
VICTOR

I REQUIRE ASSISTANCE.
(I need help.)

W · — —
WHISKEY

I REQUIRE MEDICAL ASSISTANCE.
(I need a doctor.)

X — · · —
X-RAY

STOP CARRYING OUT YOUR
INTENTIONS.
(Don't do what you are doing.)

Y — · — —
YANKEE

I AM DRAGGING MY ANCHOR.
(My anchor is in the water
behind my moving boat.)

Z — — · ·
ZULU

I REQUIRE A TUG.
(I need someone to push me.)

Blocks A, B, M, V and Z are the most DIFFICULT ones to
make. Save them for AFTER you have practiced on lots
of EASIER patchwork flags. Assembly diagrams are on
page 39 and are included on the pattern sheets. Block "I"
is appliquéd. Page 33 shows you how.

MAKE PATCHWORK ALPHABET BLOCK TEMPLATES

Follow the instructions for template making on the pattern sheets that came in the kit.

Make blocks with squares and rectangles the same way you made the FOUR PATCH BLOCK.

C, D, E, G, H, J, K, L, Q, T and U are EASIEST to do. R and X are simple too:

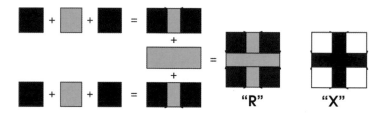

P and S both use the same shapes.

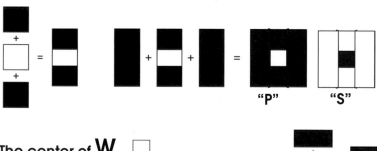

The center of **W** is a BLOCK like an "S" block made with smaller pieces.

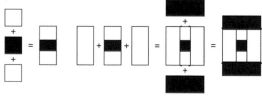

"W"

NOTE: The pattern sheets for these alphabet blocks are included in the *My First Patchwork Book* kit, or you may order them at www.palmerpletsch.com.

Template plastic, instead of poster board, will make the best templates for these alphabet projects.

N uses 16 squares made using a 3½" SQUARE TEMPLATE.

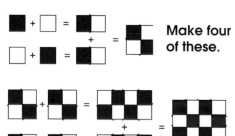

Make four of these.

"N"